DENBIGH

A Pictorial History
Volume 3

by
R.M. Owen

This volume is dedicated to Rachel whose tolerance of my passion for local history became legendary.

FOREWORD

It gives me great pleasure to write the foreword for this long awaited third volume of the Pictorial History of Denbigh. Not only are the photographs interesting in their own right but to the historian, they reflect further aspects of the social, religious, political and commercial development of the town.

Denbigh is fortunate in having someone who is not only enthusiastic about the town and its history but who is always willing to share his comprehensive knowledge in this field. We are much enriched by this and are indebted to R M Owen for his time, effort and meticulous research in preparing this volume and for sharing with us another instalment of his unique collection of photographs.

Such a contribution enables us to further enjoy and understand the rich heritage of our ancient and fascinating town. This volume will certainly be cherished and will give many people much pleasure and information. I sincerely hope that the author will continue to publish and share with us the wealth of his knowledge of local history.

Gwyn Jones, Llannefydd.

INTRODUCTION

A further accumulation of postcards and other photographs has provided both the stimulation and opportunity to compile a third representation of the Pictorial History of Denbigh.

Our older inhabitants have witnessed several architectural and social changes and these have not all necessarily resulted in an improvement to the town. Nevertheless it is hoped that the contents of this volume will not only be the means of providing a nostalgic trip into the past but will also give inspiration to generations as yet unborn to continue recording our history.

I must avail myself of this opportunity to express my sincere thanks to those who, mindful of the need to preserve old pictures and documents, have made them readily available for research and recording.

I wish also to thank Medwyn Jones for typing the script.

Whereas the sequence of pictures in previous volumes was arranged as a town trail, on this occasion they are shown in chronological order, thus reflecting, to some extent, the changes and events as they occurred.

St David's Church, 1841. The present St David's Church, now in the care of Howell's School, is the second church erected on this site. The earlier church, shown above, was built between 1838 and 1840 on land presented by Captain Mostyn of Segrwyd and consecrated by Bishop Carey on 13th December 1840. It consisted of a nave with galleries, a small apse and a vestry. Due to a combination of structural faults and a measure of subsidence, this church was demolished in 1894, but the tower, shorn of its spire, was incorporated into the new cruciform church which we have today.

Vale Street c 1880

The grocer's shop on the left later became the Free Press Office; the National Provincial Bank, now the National Westminster Bank, was built in 1850 on the site previously occupied by the Leopard Inn before its removal to High Street; the grocer's shop known as Littler and Williams was later taken over by Christmas Lewis, another grocer; the next shop, once known as Bric á Brac, was until recent years owned by Aled Owen, newsagent. St Thomas's Church, the spire of which is a prominent landmark, had been erected 16 years before this photograph was taken. Most of the architectural features of the street remain, except for the removal of the iron railings during World War II for salvage purposes.

Eisteddfod Genedlaethol
Dinbych 1882

1882 National Eisteddfod. August 22nd – 26th.

The pavilion, designed by R Lloyd Williams, was erected on the sloping land below the Royal Bowling Green, near the Castle. Measuring 165ft by 105ft, it was divided into three bays with accommodation for 6,500 people. To safeguard the finances, 150 townspeople entered into a covenant of £5 each. The Gorsedd ceremony was held on the Castle Green with Clwydfardd of Denbigh as Archdruid. The Chairman of the Executive Committee was J Harrison Jones, Chemist; Secretary E Mills and Treasurer J Robinson, North Wales Hospital. Several downpours of torrential rain caused great inconvenience – those at the rear of the pavilion have opened their umbrellas!

High Street c 1886

This tranquil, sunlit, scene almost entirely free from vehicular traffic, reflects the peace of a bygone age. The donkey cart and handcart to the rear are parked without fear of causing an obstruction as the photographer carefully arranges the people to pose for his camera. The Town Cross (1848) was the fourth market cross to be erected over the centuries. The Piazza (Y Bylciau), with the pillars supporting the upper floors of the buildings, is an unique architectural feature of Denbigh and well merits its listed status. The building in the far distance, E P Jones, Grocer, was demolished in 1891 prior to the building of the Conservative Club.

High Street Pump c 1890

This is probably the clearest photograph of the old High Street pump. Here, before the availability of a mains water supply, the inhabitants of the area would come for their daily requirements. The quality of water available was poor and conducive to frequent outbreaks of disease. Other contemporary sources of water were the wells at Barker's Well, Charnell's Well, Carter's Well, Bronyffynnon and Goblin Well. The shop adjacent, now Siop Clwyd, was then known as Siop Pwmp. On the south side of the street, to the left of the Vaults, is T. J. Williams, Drapery, (now Boots, Chemist), which was sold about 1900 to Messrs Denson of Chester

Crown Square c.1892

This large crowd had gathered to hear the announcement of the general Election result for the constituency of West Denbigh – either July 1892 or July 1895. A poster on the gable end of the County Hall solicits support for Roberts. This would be John Herbert Roberts, later Lord Clwyd, (1863 – 1955) who was Liberal member for the constituency from 1892 to 1918. Dating the picture is facilitated by the Cross Keys Inn (demolished 1903), which can be seen beyond the Town Cross. The pillared north wall of the County Hall gave a fair measure of light to the stallholders who traded on the ground floor.

The Leopard Inn c.1895

This picture of the Leopard Inn on High Street is earlier than that shown in Volume 1. The landlord, A Correll, held the licence in 1895 and is seen standing near the doorway. CADW have listed the building as Grade II and whilst the façade has changed completely, the upper floor windows remain the same. The Free Press of the 23rd May 1909 reports that following purchase by Robert Owen, grocer, and reconstruction by Walter Wheeler, builder, of Love Lane, the premises became, 'two shops, one of which was the Pioneer Drapery and the other W Davies, Dyers and Cleaners'. Currently the shop is known as The Patchwork Cat.

Love Lane Garage c.1904

This 10 HP Benz Petrol Motor Engine was first registered on the 23rd December, 1903, the original owner being Elliot Scott Correy of Fachlwyd Hall, Cyffylliog. On 5th January, 1912 it was bought by David Cushion of Well Street, Ruthin and by 7th April, 1912 remodelled and registered as a lorry. Here it is shown outside the Love Lane Garage of the Williams Brothers (Est. 1858), seen here standing to the rear of the vehicle, with the Britannia Inn to the right. They were coachbuilders of high repute employing carpenters, wheelwrights, painters and blacksmiths and probably built the coachwork on a company provided chassis.

Crown Lane c.1904

This unique picture shows Crown Lane before the demolition of the buildings on the left which preceded the building of the present Town Hall in 1916. Prior to its purchase by the Borough Council in 1904, the Farmers Arms was one of the largest inns in the town. Up to 1857 it was known as the Three Wolves Heads and housed a well-known theatre. On the right hand side the buildings would have been from right to left – Mellards Warehouses, Old Butchers Arms (closed 1908), New Butchers Arms (closed 1904) and Robert Ellis, butcher who was followed by Parry Jones, Penybryn.

May Day 1904

This entry by the Royal Daylight American Oil Company has just been awarded first prize for a decorated horse drawn cart at the Denbigh May Day Festivities. The R.D.A.O.C was the forerunner of the Esso Petroleum Company. Holding the reins is Eddie Edwards (grandfather of Ron Edwards) who for many years was local manager of the branch. Paraffin was in great demand for domestic lighting and heating purposes and in accordance with local custom he was dubbed Eddie Paraffin. This picture was taken in the Vale of Clwyd Timber Yard, now Townsend Supplies, with the gable end of Abbey Terrace in the distance.

Bull Hotel c.1905

Listed as Grade II* the Bull Hotel is Denbigh's most historic inn. The original building, the triple gabled section to the right, has an Early Tudor core, but the section to the left, with a shaped gable bearing the hotel name, is of the late 17th century. Originally a town house, this part was at one time Fairholme School until it was incorporated into the Bull. At the top of Park Street is the entrance to the Fire Station, which was based in the hotel yard from 1897 until 1917, during which time, Robert Lloyd, the proprietor, was Brigade Captain.

Frongoch School c.1905

In 1876 the School Board of Denbigh purchased from John Richard Heaton 'part of a field called Tanyfron adjoining Red Lane at a price of 2s 6d per yard', the purpose being the building of an Infants' School. In 1895 this was extended to include a Girls' School. Love Lane Boys' School closed in 1938 and Frongoch then became a Junior Mixed School. In 1973 the Infants moved to their new school at Ysgol y Parc. Since 1986 the buildings at Grove Road have been re designed as an Area Magistrates' Court and the school transferred to the former Ysgol y Dyffryn Special School on Rhyl Road.

Park Street c.1905

Apart from the cobbled pavements and gutterways, there seems to have been little architectural change to Park Street during the past century. Two years previously, Plas Coch, the building on the right, housed the Denbigh Grammar School before the erection of the new County School in Middle Lane. The knickerbockers, Eton collars and caps of the boys and the smocks and hats of the girls are typical Edwardian dress. The telegram boy on the right and the milkman with his float in the middle distance are also relics of a bygone age.

PARK St. DENBIGH

May Pole Dancing 1905

The preparation of the school children for the annual May Pole dancing at the castle was entrusted to D Harry Hughes, assistant at the Boys' National School and Miss Watkin, headmistress of the Girls' National School. The practices were held at the Memorial Hall (now Theatr Twm o'r Nant) with Minnie Batten as accompanist. Harry Hughes, secretary of the Literary Society and of Denbigh FC later became headmaster of Chirk School. On his retirement, he returned to Denbigh to keep the fishmonger's shop where Clough's offices are now. Miss Watkin left the school when she married J Hughes, owner of the wool shop, now Ariel Travel.

Denbigh
Whitchurch, Interior

St Marcella's Church 1907

This is the interior of Whitchurch before the major restoration undertaken in 1908 at a cost of £1,900. The works included excavation of the floor and the removal of the enclosed pews and their replacement with a block floor and movable chairs. The new chancel screen was rebuilt from parts of the old screen at the rear of the church. In the Chancel itself, the candelabra from St Hilary's was rehung and stalls provided. The tower was redesigned as a vestry and all the church monuments were restored and some re-positioned. The whole roof was uncovered and the timbers bolted and secured.

Denson's Furnishing Department 1907

Densons Drapery (now Boots Chemist) came to Denbigh c 1900 when T J Williams retired from his drapery business. The furnishings department was located in Broomhill Lane to the rear of Andrews Vaults and was connected to the main shop both by an underground tunnel and by an overhead covered passageway spanning the lane. Most householders floored their rooms with linoleum, a material sold in rolls as shown here. Linoleum consisted of a canvas backing coated with a preparation of linseed oil and powdered cork which could be worked into a highly polished surface. Note the chairs carefully arranged for the customer's use.

Denbigh Fire Brigade Outside Bull Hotel, 1908

In 1858 the Borough Council first established a Fire Brigade. For 20 years the engine was housed in the Vegetable Market but following several disputes between the Authority and the Brigade members, the Station was moved to the Bull Hotel Yard. In 1917, the next move was to the Crown Lane side of the newly built Town Hall. Until 1923, the engine was still horsedrawn and in 1928 a two bay Fire Station was erected on the Town Hall car park. In 1941, the Fire Services were nationalised and the present Station in Smithfield Road was built in 1970.

May Day 1910

May Day was traditionally a day of celebration in Denbigh. Featured here in Vale Street, is one of my grandfather's (John Morris Owen) wagons with his carter, John Williams, at the horse's head. The children of Post Office Lane in their Eton collars are dressed for the occasion and the horse is resplendent in its brasses and plaited tail and mane. The ivy clad building to the rear is currently occupied by Jones Peckover, Land Agents but was previously the office of Goronwy Griffiths, Architect and before that the residence of Dr J Lloyd Roberts, son of the Rev R J Roberts who was Rector of Denbigh from 1843 to 1855.

Free Press Office c. 1910

The Free Press was first published on the 25th June 1881 by Charles Cottom, (1844 – 1925), seen here fourth from left. The first premises were almost opposite to Bronallt in upper Vale Street, the home of his rival printer and publisher, Thomas Gee, before the flourishing business moved to 33, Vale Street. Cottom's venture, being supportive of Toryism and the Established Church, was in direct contrast to the well-established Radicalism of Gee's Press in Swan Lane. In 1957 the Free Press acquired the copyright of the North Wales Times. In recent times Vale Clocks occupied these premises.

Grove Road 1910

As far back as 1610, Grove Road, because of the sandy nature of the soil, was known as Red Lane and the Welsh version, Lôn Goch, is still used by older Denbighites. The Ordnance Survey maps for 1874 show two working sandpits near the junction with Middle Lane. The names Elm Villas, Grove Terrace and Grove Road are misguided attempts by the Borough Council of 1900 to give an air of Anglicised Victorian grandeur to the road. Despite the steepness of Beacon's Hill and Grove Road, this was a favoured pedestrian route to and from the station, which can be seen in the middle distance.

Good Templars Funeral 1912

Seen here on Denbigh High Street is the lengthy cortège at the funeral of Mrs Hughes known as Mrs Hughes Ysbrydion. She lived at Gallt y Coed, Vale Street and on the wall above a fireplace were inscribed the words 'Heb Dduw, Heb Ddim, Duw a Digon'. She was a strong advocate of Temperance and a leading member of the Caledfryn Lodge of Good Templars. These mourners are wearing their regalia and silk hats and in the middle distance is the horse-drawn hearse. The interment took place at Henllan and the large turnout is an indication of the respect in which she was held.

Territorial Camp 1913

These Territorials have disembarked from their troop train at Denbigh Station and are en route to Myddleton Park where the Liverpool Infantry Brigade was encamped. The locals, seen in the background regarded the arrival of these troops as an event of great excitement. To the right are Gladstone Villas (erected 1882), opposite the Railway Inn. At this time, any form of mechanisation of the armed forces was in its infancy and no doubt successive improvements had transformed the bicycle from an amusing toy to an article of general utility, with a potential for use in situations of war.

Denbigh Station 1913

This superb postcard by the Carbonora Company of Liverpool was posted from Denbigh on 22nd August, 1913 to Miss L McDougall of 23, Park View, Crosby. 'A.G' who sent the card said that they were 'having a splendid time but that climbing the hills was dreadful'. This detachment of the Liverpool Scottish, resplendent in their kilts, tartan forage caps, stockings and gaiters has just alighted from their train on the Chester platform. Within 12months, World War 1 had begun and it is a matter of conjecture how many of these reservists survived the holocaust.

Ruthin Road 1913

Under the Territorial training facilities organised at Denbigh, the Liverpool Scottish occupied Myddleton Park, the Army Service Corps were based on a field opposite Myddleton Park, the Artillery were in the two fields near Cotton Hall on the Llandyrnog Road and the YMCA headquarters were located at the junction of the roads leading to Ruthin and Llandyrnog. Drilling took place on the four fields below St Marcella's Church. The Ordnance Stores, as can be seen in this picture by Helsby, were situated on the field between Plas Pigot and the turning to Ystrad Road, where the gable end of Glyn Garth can be seen.)

Roman Catholic Tent 1913

Each of the religious denominations in Denbigh was eager to cater for the spiritual needs of its own members at the Territorial Camp and as shown here, the local Catholic Church was no exception. Father Raymond Barker, standing beside the altar, was priest at Denbigh from 1907 apart from the war years (1914 – 1919) until 1932 when he was succeeded by Father Earle and then Father Cubbly who left at the end of the Second World War. Father Barker himself sent this postcard to a Mrs Williams of Nantglyn, who was a patient at the Royal Alexandra Hospital in Rhyl.

Denbigh Christmas Show. 1913.

Eglwys Wen Farm 1913.

These prize winners at the Smithfield 1913 Christmas Show were sold by Griffith Jones to the following butchers – Thomas Davies, 2, Vale Street, £29-5s-0d; J W Davies, 92 Vale Street, £25-5s-0d; H Dryhurst Roberts, Market Hall, £22-10s-0d; and R Hughes, Trawsfynydd £24-5s-0d. The main prize, a silver cup given by the Mayor, Thomas Lloyd Jones, was awarded to Thomas Jones, Brondyffryn Farm and the animal sold to H Parry Jones, butcher, Crown Lane for £45. During the 19th century, Eglwys Wen Farm, owned by H R Hughes, Kinmel Hall, was let to Thomas Gee, the publisher. Using a telescope from his home, Bronallt he was said to check on the movements of his employees.

Recruiting Parade 1914

With the dark clouds of World War 1 looming, the Government encouraged the promotion of recruiting drives. The Volunteers were already committed to war service but general conscription was not enforced until January 19th 1916. Standing at the base of the Town Cross is the Mayor, T Lloyd Jones. To the rear the old Town Markets have been demolished and the New Town Hall is in the course of construction. On the left is Dicks Cash Boot Stores and on the right W Clwyd Pierce's delicatessen followed by Star Tea Company and then the Crown Hotel where the landlord was Robert Hughes.

Sunday Schools rally c. 1914

The streets are thronged with participants and spectators at this District Sunday Schools Rally. The second banner from the left is that of Bontuchel Band of Hope, theirs being the earliest Calvinistic Methodist Chapel in the area. To the rear is the Town Band which escorted the parade to the castle where a programme of hymn singing was arranged. The children were then entertained to tea at the various chapel schoolrooms. Shops to the right of the County Hall are – John Thomas, Clothier; The Post Office; Harrison Jones, Chemist and Bradleys, Outfitters. On the advertising boards is the stark message, ' The Curse of War'.

Denbighshire Yeomanry 1914

This group includes Ruthin and Denbigh members of the Denbighshire Yeomanry in the yard of the Talbot Hotel (now Forum Restaurant) at the outbreak of World War 1 (1914-1918). Before the creation of the Factory Ward car park, the yards of the Back Row (now Eagles), Talbot, White Lion and Golden Lion extended to the roadway, thus Pendref Chapel can be seen beyond the yard doors. In the group are the licensee of the Talbot, Mrs Grace Hall and her daughter. In late 1916, the Denbighshire Yeomanry was dismounted and absorbed into the 24th Battalion, Royal Welsh Fusiliers.

Glas Meadows 1917

This sequel to the threshing scene at Bryn y Ffynnon in Henllan Street shown in Volume 1 depicts the same machine having moved to the field known as Glas Meadows. In the background are the castle ruins and the roof of the former Pendref smallholding. Glas Meadows was rented out by the Town Council as part of an agricultural holding with occasional lettings for travelling circuses. In winter time it was a favourite venue for sledging. Since the 1930s provision has been made for the letting of garden allotments and the erection of headquarters for a Rifle Club and the Air Training Corps.

Miller's Glass and China Stores 1918.

This shop, known as Chirbury House in Back Row, now a vacant office, occupied the site of the old Feathers Inn which was demolished in 1845 when the old Borough Markets were built. To the left can be seen the sign of the Back Row Hotel (now Eagles), then owned by Pryce Storey of Coppy Farm. Sam Miller specialised in the sale of Goss Crested Ware which he displayed separately in the three cabinets. The sign above the shop entrance indicates that he was also a parcels agent for the London and North Western Railway.

Fron Shop c. 1920

This popular grocery stores on Rhyl Road was opened to cater for the needs of the expanding Townsend district. A typical conversion from house to shop premises, there was a bakehouse at the rear which customers made use of to roast poultry and joints of meat. The custom of displaying hams and sides of bacon outside the shop would not conform with current hygiene regulations. Standing second from the right is David Edward Williams (Dei Pop), probably the finest all-round cricketer produced in the area. Despite several offers to turn professional, he preferred to remain with the town club.

Tanswan Shop c1920

Following a disastrous fire in 1982 by which time it had become a greengrocers shop, the above grocers was demolished. Owned initially by Mr T A Roberts, it was known as Siop Tanswan because the business originated in Vale Street, below the Swan Inn (presently HSBC Bank). Mr Roberts, who was succeeded by his daughter, was a devout Christian and a deacon at Capel Mawr. At 8am daily, it was his custom to invite any passer by to join him and his staff in a religious service. Miss Roberts, a talented musician in her own right, had several pupils, including the famous soprano, Madam Laura Evans.

Abbey Garage, 1920

Abbey Garage was built by the Ford Motor Company in 1920 for William Edwards, the other site at the end of Garden Terrace being too restricted. With his brother Bob Edwards (Enterprise Stores, High Street), William Edwards formed the Red Dragon Bus Company. Charlie Lightning and Evan Pierce (both later at Crown Garage), were employed as mechanics and Harry Ellis as clerk. By 1930 the company had 12 licenced buses running local routes with sufficient staff to run The Red Dragons Football team. The Crosville Bus Company had already bought out the White Rose Bus Company and three months later the Red Dragon was also taken over.

Isaac Morris, Shoemaker c.1920
Seen in the doorway of his shop in Swine Market, clad in his leather apron, is Isaac Morris, a well respected Denbighite and deacon at Capel Seion, Henllan Street. His first-born son, Richard Morris, became Liberal MP for Battersea North and was with Lloyd George at the signing of the Treaty of Versailles in 1919. Two other sons emigrated to Australia and the business passed to his protégé, Llewelyn Bartley who continued in the same trade for many years. The shoe repairing tradition has been maintained here by the Cawthray family who previously had shops successively at Vale Street, High Street, Hall Square and Bridge Street.

The National School c.1920

The National School in Lenten Pool was built in 1847 to success the old Bluecoat School, founded in 1714 and located in Highgate. Prominent among former headmasters is John Williams (Glanmor) 1811 – 1891, the author of several books including Ancient and Modern Denbigh and The Records of Denbigh and its Lordship. Originally a Boys' School, the section to the right formed the School House with the re shaped entrance seen as the second window from the right. With the opening of Ysgol Heulfre, the school closed in 1976 and the facade has been preserved as the front of a complex of flats for the elderly.

Hawk Villa c. 1920

Hawk Villa in Post Office Lane was the home of Sergeant Hawke who came to Denbigh as an instructor to the local Volunteers. It was subsequently the home of Charles Evans a book-keeper at Gwasg Gee. Having a rather aquiline nose he became known as Hawk Eye. Later, Tom Wynne, shoemaker at Hall Square lived here. To the right is the entrance to the Hawk and Buckle yard. Contrary to popular belief, there has never been a Crown Post Office in the area. The street name is derived from Posting House, i.e. where coach horses were changed in the inn yard.

Staff of Denbigh County School c.1922

On the front steps of the County School (opened 1903) in Middle Lane are the headmaster and his staff. From left to right – Edward Ellis Jones, who was later ordained priest and taught Welsh and Latin; Rev D E Jenkins, former pastor of St Thomas' Church and then Geography Master; L Stanley Jones, History Master; D H Davies, Headmaster from 1898 to 1925; J T Jones, Classics Master and lay preacher who subsequently became headmaster of Ruabon Grammar School; unknown; J W Askew, Chemistry Master. J T Jones and J W Askew were founder members of the Denbigh Literary Society while Edward Jones and Stanley Jones were prominent Freemasons.

St Hilary's Church 1923

Erected during the 14th century, St Hilary's was replaced gradually by St David's (1841) and St Mary's (1874). The building fell into disrepair and in 1923 it was demolished, public protests having secured the retention of the tower. The contractor, William Ellis of Panton Hall, used the stones, slates and timbers to erect a new house – Coriander at the top of New Road. The pendant brass candelabrum (1752), a communion table (1623), and a bell (1683) were transferred to St Marcellas's and some of the woodwork was used to furnish St Andrew's Mission Church. Several Denbigh families claim to have articles fashioned from the ruins.

Territorials Camp 1924

This group of RWF Territorials at their annual camp shows members of several well-known Denbigh families whose descendants are still resident in the area. Back row, L to R, Griff the Green, an outstanding middleweight boxer who once achieved a draw with Jack McAvoy, the British champion; Ted Coope, Tom Frimstone, Bob Jones (Ginger); Front row L to R, Dick Barnett, Richard David Williams, C Wills and George Conway Williams. The weekly activities at the Drill hall and the annual camp provided a most acceptable diversion from the humdrum of daily routine and were also the source of a small but regular income.

Motor Garage, Vale Road c 1925

From the Abbey Garage on Rhyl Road (1920), William Edwards ran the Red Dragon Bus Service. Here, near Garden Terrace, he had already established a motor repair business. The advertisements proclaim the merits of Dunlop Tyres, Vacuum Mobiloils and Pratts finest American Lamp Oil. The open top car with the spare wheel on the running board, the motorcycle with side-car and the solitary gas lamp are all reminiscent of a bygone age. In recent years Elfed Evans continued the garage business and it was here that Kwik Save opened their first Denbigh store. The premises are now owned by Copyrite.

Vale Street 1925

This rather bleak scene shows R G Jones' Drapers Shop during a Great Dispersal Sale. These premises were subsequently occupied by W H Smith Newsagents and then Cronins. The shop on the left was Clwyd Pierce's Delicatessen prior to Hepworths Drapers taking it over. On the right is the old Gas Shop, currently an accountants office. The posters on top of the hoarding advertise a Welsh League match between Denbigh United and Mold. The North Wales Times announces Lloyd George's visit to Caerwys and Baner Cymru proclaims a Disservice to Wales. Below it is stated that during alterations, business will be as usual at David Knowles Drapery.

The Mission Church c1925

St Andrew's in Henllan Street, a corrugated iron church, opened in 1907 during the rectorship of Canon Redfern. The interior has been specially decorated for the Harvest Fstival Service which was traditionally held in Welsh as were all the evening services thus reflecting the Welshness of Henllan Street at that time. The altar rails were constructed from those at St Hilary's which had recently been demolished. The centre piece of the altar, The Good Shepherd, was adapted as a War Memorial to those members who were killed in the two World Wars and is now in St Mary's Church.

Argoed, Beacon's Hill c1925

Argoed (now Gwyfan) the spacious villa, which stands almost opposite the entrance to Post Office Lane, was adapted from being a residence to accommodate Fairholme School when it moved from 57, Vale Street. Partners in the school were Mrs Ceridwen Lloyd and her sister, Miss Evadne Ffoulkes. By 1932 it had become the manse for the Capel Mawr minister, Rev J H Griffith and the school moved to Lôn Copner, before moving again in 1945 to Pilkington House, St Asaph. When J H Griffith moved to the new manse in Lôn Llewelyn, he took the name Argoed with him.

Lôn Llewelyn 1927/28

Shown here are the workmen responsible for erecting the council houses on the lower section of Lôn Llewelyn. Denbighites seen in the back row include – Bob Richards, Hugh Richards, Tom Pierce, Will Pierce and Robert William Pierce. At the right end of the front row are Isaac Davies and Baden Roberts. Before this, council houses had already been built at – Smithfield Road in 1927, Maes Hyfryd in 1924 and Myddleton Avenue in 1926. They were followed by Henllan Street in 1929 and 1933, Clwyd Avenue in 1930, Lloyds Avenue in 1931, Maes Glas in 1937 and Maes y Dre in 1938/39.

VIEW FROM DENBIGH CASTLE.

Waterworks House and reservoir 1927

This panoramic view shows clearly the council dwellings in Myddleton Avenue (built 1925) and Lower Lôn Llewelyn, (built 1927). In the foreground is the water storage tank and the old Waterworks House where Edward Hughes, Y Dŵr, lived. This house was rebuilt in the 1930s when Percy Freeman was appointed waterman. Water was pumped over two miles from Llwyn Isaf Waterworks and to a height of 350 feet to this reservoir, which had been constructed in 1864 to provide water for the newly opened Vale of Clwyd Railway. In 1937 an additional reservoir was built on the land fronting Denbigh Castle.

George Price Davies
(1904 – 1988) 1928

Griff y Grîn and George Price Davies, shown above, were the best known of a succession of Denbigh boxers. The training quarters were in a room behind the Hawk and Buckle Inn with Cliff Chinnery as trainer. George Davies achieved his greatest success when in 1928, despite the disability of a withered right leg, a handicap he had carried from birth, he became the North Wales Flyweight Champion. He developed incredible defensive qualities and, while standing on a handkerchief, would challenge sparring partners to attempt to strike him. A notebook containing the record of his boxing career is in the possession of Sparrow Harrison, Cae Dai.

Myddleton's Newsagents, 1928

Seen here are Mr and Mrs D.C. Hughes, proprietors of the well-known newsagents, tobacconists and confectioners shop at the junction of High Street with Rosemary Lane which flourished in Denbigh for many years. The newspaper placards of *The Mirror, Herald* and *News Chronicle* are prominent and there are two advertisements for *Almanac Caergybi* 1928. Popular brands of tobacco shown are *Cymro Dewr, Three Castles, Rajah* and *Gold Flake*. Pre 1900 the premises were occupied by R.W. Jones, Ironmonger and before that the famous Green family had a similar business. Below the shop is a cellar where paraffin and lamp oil were stored. Currently the owners are Corbetts, bookmakers.

Bridge Street c1928

Dei Bassett, a local solicitor's clerk is shown here walking down Bridge Street, which, over the centuries has been variously named – Chappelle Lane, Lôn Sowter and Portland Place. The buildings shown, from L to R are – Hennessey Terrace, built for a Mrs Hennessey as a wedding gift from her father; The Plough Inn listed Grade II as having late-medieval timber-framed origins and the workshops of James Jones, cabinet maker. Across the road – Anwyl Hughes wool shop where, to much consternation in the town the proprietor hanged himself in the upper room; Gresley's electrical shop and John Roberts saddlery.

The Black Lion c1928

Seen here in a dilapidated condition, prior to its demolition, is the old Black Lion Inn in Henllan Street. The earliest reference to the inn is an assessment of 1768 and it closed in 1853, becoming a dwelling house, In 1928, Hugh Lloyd Jones, Builder erected the present 7 houses on the site. From the right the buildings were occupied by – John Jones, (Jack y Big); Black Lion (gabled); parlour of Black Lion; Robert Jones, (tanner); vehicular entrance to the inn yard and John Gallimore (sweep). The land behind the inn where Maes y Goron was built was known as Black Lion fields.

Vale of Clwyd Timber Company 1928.

For centuries the woodlands of the Vale of Clwyd have produced an abundance of timber. The haulage to the timber yard was by horse and wagon and the sawing carried out in saw-pits. This picture shows D Gwilym Lloyd at the Town Saw Mills where by this time a horizontal saw bench had been installed. His father, Dafydd Llwyd, a well known character, had been involved in the business since the late 19th century but by 1915 he was in partnership with H M Lewis, who was Mayor of Denbigh from 1945-1946. Dafydd Llwyd and Gwilym Lloyd were prominent members at Capel Bodawen, now a nursery school.

May Day 1929

This gaily-bedecked Vulcan Lorry parked in Barker's Well Lane was an entry for decorated motor vehicles at the 1929 May Day festivities. The owner of the vehicle, George Pierce, was a well-known Denbigh contractor. The people shown from left to right are – Trefor Jones, (driver); Jack Williams, known as Jack Fron Gelen, (bus driver); Emyr Peters, (later Assistant Chief Nursing Officer at the North Wales Hospital); Wilfred Royles, (taxi proprietor) and R H Lloyd, (later Post Master) with Beryl Pierce, George Pierce's daughter on the lorry little realising that in 5 years time she would be May Queen.

Galch Hill c1930

Galch Hill, a junior house to Gwaenynog in the Myddleton line, dates from the late 16th century. Richard Myddleton (1508 – 1575) was Governor of Denbigh Castle and among his nine sons born here and commemorated by the Myddleton Plaque in St Marcella's Church were – Sir Hugh Myddleton (1560 – 1631) whose New River Scheme brought water to London and Sir Thomas Myddleton (1550 – 1631), Lord Mayor of London 1613, who in 1595 established the Myddleton dynasty at Chirk Castle. The name Galch Hill may be derived from the German 'Galgenhugel' – Gallows Hill – but it is more likely to have originated from a geological characteristic.

May Day 1932

Seen at the Infirmary is the 1932 May Queen, Alice Welburn, a 13-year-old pupil at the National School, of Groes Hall Cottage. Her attendants were Hazel Emmanuel and Joan Dominey with Megan Williams at the rear. The pages were Kenneth Ellis and E A Gorham, son of the curator of the Conservative Club who was joint secretary of the event. Messrs Densons Drapers supplied the crown and the gowns were made by Miss Walker, Vale Street and Mrs Dominey, Maes Hyfryd. The procession formed in Lenten Pool then proceeded via Vale Street to Middle Lane for the crowning ceremony.

Hoisting the Red Dragon 1933

On the 27th May 1933, the secretary of the Welsh Nationalist Party – West Denbigh Branch – wrote to thank Robert Davies, Town Clerk for the Council's support of a request to fly the Welsh Dragon at Denbigh Castle. Here the Mayor, Councillor John Morris Jones is at the flagstaff accompanied by, among others, 1st, 4th and 6th from the right respectively – Harry Jones, who was himself subsequently Town Clerk, Councillor J H Mills and R Kerfoot Owen, Smithfield Garage. John Morris Jones, during a lifetime of public service was, - Mayor of Denbigh (1933 – 35), Minister of Waen Chapel, Editor of *Y Faner*, Chief Templar of Wales and Secretary to Denbigh Infirmary.

The Silver Penny c.1934

Grouped on the vestry stage after a performance of The Silver Penny are the Sunday School members of Capel Seion (Capel Bach) in Henllan Street. Seated in the front, from left to right are - Mr Evans (Postman Bach); Rev John Hughes; Miss Jinnie Williams, (Gas Office); and Mr Pugh Davies (Gee's Press). Standing on the left is Mr Robert Owen, (grocer). Taking the principal role and standing in the rear is Gwyneth Griffiths, (now Wynne). For over a century Capel Seion (1856), built as a daughter chapel to Capel Mawr, played a prominent part in the religious and cultural life of Upper Denbigh.

Silver Jubilee 1935

Union Jacks are prominent in this Silver Jubilee scene on Denbigh High Street. Close inspection reveals one Stars and Stripes but not a single Draig Goch! Following the 25 years reign of George V and Queen Mary, councils throughout the land organised celebrations whereby school children were presented with bronze medals and commemorative mugs. In the foreground is schoolboy Howel Idris Jones, then of Pendref, Love Lane. E B Jones, Grocers, now Holland and Barrett stood on the site of the Three Boars Heads Inn, which was closed in 1854. The balcony of the Liberal Club was a popular vantage point, from which to view street processions.

Astons Furniture Stores c.1935

Currently occupied by furnishers Happy Homes, this imposing building was the 18th century dower house owned by the Heaton family and known as Tŷ Mawr. The conversion to commercial premises was carried out by publisher Thomas Gee. Astons, with its headquarters at Wrexham, did a brisk trade and many local households were furnished from its ample stocks. Seen here in one of the display rooms are – left to right – Ronald Thompson, photographer who had bought Helsby's business nearby; Dilys Williams, wife of John Hywel Williams the pharmacist; J W Thomas, the manager and Phyllis Jones. Thompson himself took this photograph by time exposure.

Hereford House, Bridge St. c1935

Hereford House was the saddler's shop of John Roberts and later of his son Jim. John Roberts came to Denbigh as a horse collar maker for Robert Roberts High Street, but left to begin his own business in an outhouse near the Hand Inn. During the 1920s he moved to Hereford House when William Roberts gave up his grocery and there established a thriving saddlery. With the decrease in horse traffic, John Roberts diversified to deal in all manner of sports goods. Until 1850 this shop was an inn known as The White Horse. It is currently the Regency Hairdressing Salon.

High Street c.1935

This scene of Denbigh High Street on a market day reflects the amount of trade done by local shopkeepers during that pre-supermarket era. The stalls in the centre of High Street and on the land fronting Millwards shows how market traders attracted shoppers to the town. The absence of yellow lines and the freedom enjoyed by motorists is another indication of the changing times. On the immediate left is the cycle shop of Emlyn Evans with the advertisement for Royal Enfield cycles. Irwins on the right came to Denbigh in 1933 and was one of twelve grocers shops on the High Street at that time.

Opening of the Lower Park Bowling Green 10.5.1935

The facilities at the Lower Park Recreation Ground were a great boon to the people of Denbigh. The playground for children, ornamental gardens with trees donated by well-wishers, tennis courts, putting green and bowling green together with a purpose built pavilion were carefully and attractively planned. The official opening of the pavilion and bowling green was performed by the Lord Lieutenant for Denbighshire, Col R W Williams Wynne, DSO. Here he is bowling the first jack watched by Robert Davies, Town Clerk and Councillor John Morris Jones, Mayor. Having reached its 70th anniversary the bowling section has developed into a leading North Wales Club.

E W Davies, Fishmonger c. 1935

Current regulations regarding food hygiene would not permit this extravagant display of Christmas poultry outside the shop of E W Davies in Back Row. The shop interior was devoted to the sale of fish which, despite a liberal use of ice, would need to be sold quickly. Together with the men's hairdressing salon of J Ellis Jones next door, the block, known as Coronation Buildings, was erected in 1897 to commemorate the Silver Jubilee of Queen Victoria. Propped against the wall near the shop entrance is the delivery bicycle. Currently, these premises are occupied by George Williams, Insurance Consultants.

Eminent Denbighites 1937

On the 15th October 1937, at a function held at the Church Institute, five eminent Denbighites were honoured by Y Gymdeithas Gymraeg. The five, seated in the front row, from left to right are – Dr J V Rees-Roberts, Harley Street specialist; Judge Sir T Artemus Jones; Dr T Gwynn Jones, the doyen of Welsh Literati; Dr W M Edwards, Chief Inspector of Schools for Wales and Mr A G Prys-Jones, a leading Anglo Welsh poet. Seated with them are Dr Kate Roberts and Mrs T Gwynn Jones. Also invited but unable to attend were Dr Taylor Jones, Professor of Moral Philosophy at Glasgow; Dr J Newton Davies, Professor of Philosophy in America and W Lloyd Davies, Harrow, Civil Servant.

Baptist Chapel Drama Group 1937

Pre-war, most nonconformist chapels in Denbigh had flourishing drama societies. Here is the Caledfryn Society from the Baptist Chapel, having presented a new four-act comedy entitled, 'Dr Jim', at the Town Hall. The performers from left to right are – Jinnie Roberts (Bwa Fflat); Glyn Jones; John Ffoulkes; Norman Freeman; Mrs Isaac Jones; George Lloyd; Alice Williams; Griff Jones (Crosville Manager); Bronwen Rogers; Moses Morris (Borough Sanitary Inspector); Mrs George Lloyd; Morris Owen (my father); May Williams (Fron Shop); William Jones; T J Roberts and the Minister, Rev J B Hughes. Bronwen Rogers, currently resident at Llanfaircaereinion, is the sole survivor.

Father Christmas 1938

This crowd of excited children has surrounded Father Christmas outside Denbigh Railway Station. He was later driven in style on a decorated cart up Vale Street to Densons Shop (now Boots Chemist). There, at the storeroom in Broomhill Lane, he distributed presents to the lucky recipients. The bowler-hatted figure on the right directing operations is Mr O E Griffiths the shop manager. These children, not one of whom is long-trousered, would now be in their seventies. The LMS notice to the right of the station entrance advertises return trips to Chester – first class 3s 11d and third class 2s 8d.

J O Thomas, Bandmaster 1938

In pre-war days, Denbigh boasted a fine Town Band and for half a century, one of the leading bandsmen was J O Thomas of Park Street. Having worked as a blacksmith at the Foundry, he then spent 30 years with the locomotive staff at Denbigh Railway Station. In 1914, aged 42, he saw active service in France with the 4th Battalion, RWF as a Pioneer Sergeant, his son Jackie, aged 17 accompanying him. He was a bandsman from boyhood having been a member of the Volunteer Band, the Mental Hospital Band and the Town Band, of which he was elected Bandmaster. His favourite instrument was the euphonium.

1939 National Eisteddfod August 10th

In this scene, The Right Honourable D Lloyd George, OM, MP, as he is described in the Official Programme, whose presence as the Afternoon President on the Thursday of the Eisteddfod had become traditional, is setting off for the Eisteddfod field. He stayed with Aneurin Evans, a local solicitor, at Whitehall, Vale Street. His address, lasting half an hour, was 'loudly applauded' and was followed by the ceremony of welcoming the Welsh from Overseas – Croesawu'r Cymry ar Wasgar. Behind the police sergeant is local character, Jack Griffiths, the coalman and with his head above the car door is Ken Ellis of Kender, Grove Road.

Civil Defence 1941

Depicted outside the Depot at 60, Vale Street are those who participated in a war time Civil Defence Exercise. On the right is M E Morris, Sanitary Inspector, while on the far left are Councillor J H Mills and beside him, without a hat, Stanley Jones, History Master at the County School, who was Chief Air Raid Warden. Among the lady ambulance drivers are Edna Davies, Joan Johnson, Eileen Gamble and Betty Kerfoot Owen. The small boy wearing a helmet is Peter Thomas who, together with Idris Davies behind him, were messengers. To the rear of the ambulance is Jack Roberts, later local Superintendent, St John's Ambulance Brigade.

Salute the Soldier Week, May 6th – 13th, 1944.

The theme of War Weapons Week, Warship Week, Red Cross and St Johns Week was continued in Salute the Soldier Week. Denbigh and the surrounding villages were set National Savings targets and the progress was recorded on the County Hall indicators. The targets – Denbigh £12,000; Llandyrnog and Llangwyfan £7,000; Llanrhaeadr £6,000; Bodfari £5,000; Trefnant £5,000; Groes and Bylchau £4,000; Henllan £4,000; Llansannan £3,500; Cefn £3,000; Llannefydd £2,000; Nantglyn £2,000 and Prion £2,000 had almost all been achieved. During the week special events including parades, dances, whist drives, brass band concerts, boxing exhibitions, American baseball and auctions were held in aid of the Welcome Home Fund.

Denbigh Football Club 1948

On Easter Monday, March 29th 1948, at the North Wales Hospital Ground, Denbigh FC played against St Bernard's FC, Birkenhead. The local team, in black and amber shirts, shown above with their opponents, referee (J E Bartley) and officials, was represented by Cyril Roberts; Gron Parry; Fred Davies; R Glyn Roberts; Elliot Hughes; Emrys Roberts; Ron Roberts; Bob Gennoe; W T Jones; C S Jones and Phil Davies. The match result was a win for Denbigh by 3 goals to 1. Prior to the main attraction witnessed by a large crowd, the mayor, Ald W D Pierce kicked off in a special match between Denbigh Ladies and Stork Margarine Ladies, Denbigh being victorious by 4 goals to 1.

Plas Pigot c.1848

The Pigots, formerly Bigots, were a Norman family who settled in the Denbigh area during the time of Henry de Lacy in the late 13th century. The present house was built about 1815 and was the birthplace of Elizabeth Parry, mother of the explorer Henry Morton Stanley. From 1850 to 1855 it was the home of Rev R J Roberts, Rector of Denbigh and then of Miss Charlotte Griffiths, a wealthy spinster, who died in 1928. Dr D G Duff, who practised from Beech House, lived there until 1945 following which Plas Pigot, in the ownership of R Evers Swindell, became a tea house. In recent years it has become a private members club.

VALE ST. DENBIGH.

Vale Street c.1948

The most nostalgic aspect of this postcard is the errand boy on his delivery bike seen carrying his box under his arm. Most provision shops employed an errand boy whose wages were often a welcome addition to a meagre family income. D Wheway Davies on the corner of Post Office Lane was the agent for the Colwyn Bay Laundry. On the immediate right, Knowles Drapery Shop, with its extensive show rooms and intricate cash system suspended from the ceiling, did a thriving trade. Church House on the lower corner of Peake's Lane was the home of the verger for St David's Church. Here also the Parish Curates were housed.

Wilfred Pickles 1950s

Older readers will recall Yorkshireman Wilfred Pickles and his popular radio show 'Have a go', in which he was assisted by his wife Mabel to whom he gave the time-honoured command, 'Give him the money Mabel'. It was first heard on the BBC Light Programme in the 1950s and ran for more than 20 years. Shown here at a Town Hall recording are those from Denbigh who took part – from left to right – Mabel Pickles, Councillor R E Rowlands (Henllan); Eunice Roberts; John Penny; Wilfred Pickles; Llewelyn Jones; Gladwen Jones and R G Jones.

Enterprise Stores c1950

Standing in the Enterprise doorway in High Street is Ifor Lloyd (Seacome) who for many years was standard-bearer for the local branch of the RAFA. The business was owned by Bob Edwards and in addition to selling tobacco and confectionery he also dealt in antiques and acted as parcels agent for the Crosville Bus Company. The shop windows and frontage were crammed with items of furniture, crockery, antiquarian books and goods of every category. He drove a hard bargain and was in keen competition with Hetty Heywood in Love Lane. This shop is now the Flower Basket.

North Wales Hospital Chimney c 1950
This prominent landmark standing over 100ft tall was built during the major extension programme of 1899. The new steam heating system was operated from the building to the right, the Chief Engineer from the late 1920s being Glyn Pritchard, Manora. Among those employed in the stoking section were Griff Richards, D G Jones (Cockney), Llewelyn Jones (Dodo), David Jones and Bernard O'Toole. Their duties included cleaning out one of the two boilers every week whilst specialists swept the chimney. Hospital reports for 1920 show that up to 3,000 tons of coal were used annually with a standing stock of 300 tons.

Townsend c1950

The railway bridge spanning the bottom of Vale Street was opened in 1862 when the Vale of Clwyd railway extended the service from Denbigh to Ruthin. Below the bridge, to the right of the double –decker bus, were the Townsend toilets, a cast iron lean-to structure which caused the Borough Council Sanitary Inspector many problems. The large advertisement reminds us of Astons House Furnishers (now Happy Homes) and the shop on the left leading to Garden Terrace, owned by Evan Jones & Sons and managed by Mr Storey Jones was best known as a sales/repair depot for bicycles.

Toc H Rally 1951

Toc H, a World War 1 inspired religious movement, came to Denbigh in 1937 and had its headquarters in an upper room behind Beech House. On 29th May 1951, a Rally was organised at Denbigh Castle, the guest of honour being Rev. P.B. (Tubby) Clayton, M.C. This picture features members and officials of the Borough Council including Hywel Owen, Mayor; Harry Jones, Town Clerk; Rev J H Griffiths, Mayor's Chaplain; Alwyn Roberts, Borough Surveyor and Harry Jones, Mace Bearer. Also seen is Stanley Jones, History Master at the County School who was a prominent member of Toc H.

War Memorial, 1951

In 1923 the old Town Cross was moved from Crown Square to form the hub of the roundabout in Lenton Pool and the War Memorial depicting The Angel of Peace by Charles Hartwell erected in its place. Following the end of the Second World War, a plaque bearing the names of those who died in that conflict was placed on the south face of the Memorial. The dedication was given by the Rev. J.H. Griffiths, chaplain to Ald. Hywel Owen, the Mayor who unveiled the plaque. Flanking J.H. Griffiths are the Standard Bearers of the R.W.F. Old Comrades Association, Edward (Tedws) Davies and the R.A.F. Association, Ifor Lloyd.

Denbigh Infirmary 1952

Television as a form of entertainment was still in its infancy until the impetus given by the impending Coronation in 1953. Here, members of the Denbigh branch of Toc H are presenting the Infirmary with a new television set. They are from left to right – Harold Humphries, Jackie Thomas, Bryn Young and Ted Thomas. Among the Infirmary representatives are – Sister Edith Williams, Mrs Ceridwen Lloyd and Sister L Jones. Toc H, which has now disbanded did a great deal of voluntary work. Many will recall how, during World War 2, they arranged transport for servicemen stranded at Rhyl and Chester railway stations.

Fire Service Funeral 1953

This unique picture taken in Rhyl Road shows the funeral of Sub Officer Robert Hugh Jones, officer in charge of the Denbigh Fire Station. The coffin was carried on the Fire Engine, the driver Wil Jenks and the bearers Tudor Cartwright, Tom Wynne, Alan Cawthray, Elwyn Parry Davies, J R Hughes and Dick Davies being local members of the Fire Brigade. The funeral which was largely attended was held at St Marcella's (Whitchurch). Mr Jones' son, the late Bobby Jones, District Officer at Pwllheli, was awarded the MBE for his services to the Fire Service.

Denbigh Friary 1954

On Saturday 17th July 1954 members of the Denbighshire Historical Society visited Denbigh. They were conducted through the ruins of the Carmelite Friary by Mr W A Evans, headmaster of Denbigh County School, seen in the left foreground, who also lectured on the history of the Friary. Denbighshire was the last of the North Wales Counties to form its own Historical Society but a great deal of useful work had been accomplished by those who were active in its promotion- H Ellis Hughes of Coedpoeth, Idwal Jones of Rhos and Frank Price Jones of Denbigh. Among local members of the Council were – Dr J G Thomas, W A Evans, Hywel Owen and Gwilym R Jones.

Welsh Guards, c1955

Here we see a troop of Welsh Guards, accompanied by their band, who visited Denbigh on a recruiting campaign. The Drill Hall (currently Pot Black Snooker Centre) was built in 1882 to replace the old Armoury in Love Lane. Here for many decades volunteers to the Territorial Army became associated with the 4th Battalion of the Royal Welsh Fusiliers. The awning on the front of the building served as a protection from inclement weather for those awaiting buses. In the middle distance are the original buildings of the Smithfield Garage which were taken down before the erection of the present garage.

Blackpool Trip c1955

This happy group of trippers was one of many outings organised by John Wellington Jones, front row, fourth from right. Others who were prominent in organising similar events were Mrs Griffith (gof) and R Kenyon Wynne, the latter specialising in football trips. Sadly, apart from a few in the rear, those shown here are now deceased but readers will glean much pleasure from identifying several well-known personalities such as Mr & Mrs T Gladstone Jones, Mr & Mrs Rowlands; Mrs Lizzie Payne; Mr & Mrs R H Williams (butcher) and others whom limitations of space do not permit naming.

Vale Street c 1955

The comparative lack of traffic enables the motorist to park along the length of Vale Street without restriction. The Kings Arms Inn on the right, now closed and scheduled for redevelopment, was first licensed in 1824 by Jane Roberts. During the 1840s the corner of the building in Melling's Lane, which linked Vale Street with Park Street, was the town Post Office. Alan Pritchard, the licensee during the 1930s used the extensive yard and stabling at the rear as a stud for shire horses. The advertisements on the left indicate the Mitre Milk Bar, now the offices of K Hugh Dodd, Estate Agents.

Sunday Schools Festival 1955

This nostalgic scene of a once popular event in the Denbigh calendar shows the District Calvinistic Methodist Sunday Schools parading at the Gŵyl Ysgol Sul. This section of the procession shows the representatives of Bodawen Sunday School with Jennie Roberts of Beacon's Hill, a faithful member, towards the rear. Behind them is the banner of Brookhouse Sunday School. The parade was followed by a competitive meeting at the Town Hall. The Church Institute which itself once housed a thriving Sunday School is now a furniture warehouse and the towering beech trees fronting St Mary's Church have been felled

Henllan Street 1958

Denbigh Historian John Williams in 1856 described Henllan Street as 'the most disreputable quarter of the town'. Up to a century ago, most of the houses were small cottages lacking any facilities and accommodating large families. Successive Borough Councils gradually enforced a policy of slum clearance, replacing them with more suitable dwellings. Here, many of the houses to the east of Capel Seion have been demolished. To the left is the frontage of Siop Bird, which served generations of the inhabitants of the upper part of the street. The chapel itself has been remodelled to include community facilities.

Eirwen's Shop 1960

This busy greengrocer's shop, presently a kebab shop, was kept by Eirwen Jones, a popular Denbigh character. She also had another shop in Townsend run by her sister Glenys. Eirwen served her apprenticeship under Hugh Thomas Davies (now M & C Roberts) and had acquired a sound knowledge of the trade. She was particularly adept at making wreaths and bouquets, often working until the early hours. Next door, Mrs K G Owen kept a confectioner's shop, having followed Len Pierce who had a similar business. Pre-war, Mrs Lloyd Jones had a ladies and gents shoe shop here which had an ornate spiral staircase leading to the upper floor.

Coopers Grocers shop c.1960

Coopers grocery chain bought out the old established business of Ashfords owned and managed by E Owen Jones. Ashfords was a high-class grocers, which had in turn taken over from a similar establishment owned by D Morgan. At this time, before the advent of supermarkets monopolised the grocery trade, customers were served personally, butter, cheese, bacon etc being cut, weighed and wrapped by the assistant. In this picture, from left to right are – Nan Williams, Robert Lloyd, Ben Smart and the manager, W B Doran. Ben Smart was the father of the late Rev R E Smart, Warden of Ruthin. Until recently, these premises were occupied by National Milk Bars.

Factory Place c1972

On the left of this picture is the original Eirianfa, one time home of Boaz Jones, candlemaker and tanner, who was Mayor of Denbigh in 1907. Later occupants were Mrs Gordon, a German dressmaker who had rooms with Mr & Mrs Evan Jones. Next door, on summer evenings, a common sight was that of Jack Griffiths, Jack y Glo, sitting on the front step, contentedly smoking his pipe and chatting with his parrot. The entrance preceding Pendref Chapel led to Wesley Yard, a court of small houses, demolished some years previously under a slum clearance order. The houses and building opposite had been cleared in the late 1960s to create Factory Ward car park.

Factory Place c1972

This photograph shows Brook Lane linking Factory Place with Barker's Well Lane at its junction with Bryn Teg Estate. On the left is the old Bottling Stores associated with Roberts Brothers and Andrews Vaults. In more recent times Eirwen Jones moved her greengrocery business there. The Morris Traveller is parked outside Millward's Bakehouse, next door to which Tom and Wilf Royles garaged their taxis. The buildings at the bottom of the lane continuing to the right up to Greenbank Terrace were the warehouses, tannery and candle factory owned by Boaz Jones of Eirianfa. This area was completely cleared to build the multi-storey car park.